AQUAPONICS FOR BEGINNERS

The Ultimate Step-by-Step Guide to Building Your Own Aquaponics Garden System to Raising Vegetables and Fish Together

© Copyright 2021 by Viktor Garden - All rights reserved.

The following Book is reproduced below with the goal of providing information that is as accurate and reliable as possible. Regardless, purchasing this Book can be seen as consent to the fact that both the publisher and the author of this book are in no way experts on the topics discussed within and that any recommendations or suggestions that are made herein are for entertainment purposes only. Professionals should be consulted as needed prior to undertaking any of the action endorsed herein.

This declaration is deemed fair and valid by both the American Bar Association and the Committee of Publishers Association and is legally binding throughout the United States.

Furthermore, the transmission, duplication, or reproduction of any of the following work including specific information will be considered an illegal act irrespective of if it is done electronically or in print. This extends to creating a secondary or tertiary copy of the work or a recorded copy and is only allowed with the express written consent from the Publisher. All additional right reserved.

Table of Contents

AQUAPONICS FOR 1

BEGINNERS 1

    INTRODUCTION 5
    CHAPTER 1: WHY AQUAPONICS 7
        How does aquaponics work? 7
    CHAPTER 2: NUTRIENT CYCLE 14
    CHAPTER 3: TYPES OF AQUAPONICS SYSTEMS 25
        MEDIA FIDDLE 25
        NUTRIENT FILM TECHNIQUES 39
        DEEP WATER COLTURE 45
        VERTICAL TOWERS 52
        DUTCH BUCKETS 66
        DTF (DEEP FLOW TECHNIQUE) 72
        WICKING BEDS ON BED LICKING 73
    CHAPTER 4: THE BENEFITS OF AQUAPONICS 84
        Why Aquaponics the Organic Aquaponics 84
        AQUAPONICS Other Benefits 85
    CHAPTER 5: ENVIRONMENTAL IMPACT 91
    CHAPTER 6: BIOLOGICAL SURFACE AREA 94
    CHAPTER 7: BIOLOGICAL FILTERS 100
        What is a biofilter? 101
        In Why Aquaponics Requires a Biofilter 103
        Benefits of using biofilter in aquaponics 104
        Important Factors 104
        Remove first 105
        Bacteria require air 105
        Fish density 106
        How does biofilter work in aquaponics? 106
        Moving bed filter 107
        Static filters 108
        Drip Filter 109
    CHAPTER 8: FISH STOCKING 111
    CHAPTER 9: FISHS 117
    CHAPTER 10: BEST PLANTS 127
    CHAPTER 11: PEST 135
    CHAPTER 12: SYSTEM DESIGN 143
    CHAPTER 13: SUMMING UP AQUAPONICS 151
    CHAPTER 14: TIPS AND TRICKS 161
        CONCLUSION 165

INTRODUCTION

Aquaponics can be a combination of aquaculture, fish and other aquatic animals, and hydroponics growing without soil. Aquaponics uses both during symbiotic combinations during which plants are fed with underwater animal discharges or wastes. In return, the vegetables clean the water going back to the fish. Along with fish and their excrement, microbes play an essential role in the nutrition of plants. These beneficial bacteria originate in the spaces between the plant roots and convert fish waste and can therefore be used to grow solids in plants. The results are an ideal collaboration between aquaculture and horticulture.

Aquaponics can be a great hope for sustainable organic crop production, aquaculture, and water consumption. The fish waste is recycled and used for plant growth rather than being dumped within the ocean. Water is reassembled during a closed system reducing the consumption of this resource.

CHAPTER 1: WHY AQUAPONICS

Aquaponics can be a combination of two words: aquaculture and hydroponics. Aquaculture means 'the growth of organisms in the water.' Hydroponics is growing plants without using soil or earth. Aquaponics is employed in agriculture by mixing both aquaculture and hydroponics so that fish can be raised and fed to plants at a similar time in the water basin.

How does aquaponics work?

Fish shell is compost for plants within the water basin. It contains many minerals such as nitrogen, potassium, phosphorus, and ammonia. These minerals are converted into nitrates that the plant will ingest. Manure is delivered through a pump that goes from one basin to the opposite. In addition to waste from fish, sometimes plants receive additional nutritional supplements such as iron, calcium, or magnesium. This process also works to purify the water.

Underwater fish causes contamination, mainly through wells. However, that contamination is gathered around the roots of the plants. Sources automatically convert bacteria that cause contamination and therefore convert waste products underwater into nitrates. As it is said, nitrates are one of the minerals that feed plants. Consequently, plants form an ideal self-purification cycle.

The benefits of Aquaponics represent a durable and rigid cycle. It has tons of advantages for farming. These are, among others.

<u>100% reuse of manure and raw materials.</u>
<u>100% organic farming.</u>
Temperature control: Basins are usually inside and can be easily controlled with a temperature controller.
Water control: Basins are usually located inside and will not suffer from (heavy) rainfall like traditional agriculture.
Water consumption is controlled; The basin always has a substantial amount of water that it needs. In comparison, general agricultural tonnage is employed for burning, weather counting.

No disturbances or holdbacks due to weeds;

Everything grows without soil.

It is a versatile system with various cool sizes to grow plants and fish; Great customization can be installed at almost any location.

This is a quick system; The plant overgrows due to the ongoing nutrition it receives.

Aquaponics requires less manual labor and has more benefits than general agriculture because it is relatively inexpensive.

It is often used not only by companies but also by individuals. The system is usually placed in any quiet place and thus creates a self-sufficient life.

Aquaponics makes it possible to be self-sufficient, even if you live in an apartment with a balcony. However, the only thing you want to try is to buy a basin with some fish and a (small) container or a second basin with plants. Therefore, between the bay and the plants, you will want to put a pump so that both can benefit from each other's nutrition. This principle is straightforward, and although this type of agriculture has been used more intensively in the last few years, the below is for hundreds of years. As an example, Japanese people have been using Koi carp in their rice fields for many years.

Fish

You cannot keep any fish during the pool for aquaponics. For example, tropical fish will not work for aquaponics because the water temperature must remain below 30 ° C. Also, the exact temperature of the basin depends on the type of fish. Here are some samples of fish that will be used for aquaponics.

Tilapia (11-17 ° C basin)
Catfish (20-24 ° C basin)
Goldfish (16-22 ° C basin)
Trout (1-22 ° C basin)

Barramundi (26-30 ° C basin)

If you wish, Use fish not just for aquaponics but also for food; use tilapia or shrimp or crayfish.

Where to build an aquaponic space?

Whether you live on a farm or within the city, you will need a little area for aquaponic space. Aquaponic does not depend on sunlight or rain and thus is often placed on a balcony or in any room inside the house.

With aquaponics, almost any vegetable can grow, but some are better than others. Green leafy vegetables such as lettuce and kale grow well in aquaponics. Also, chilly, tomato and sweet potato are known to increase at certain times. Among fruits, strawberries grow the simplest in an aquaponic space. Basil is most suitable for herbs. Whenever you start growing vegetables, fruits, or herbs, you want to make sure that there are many mature plants inside the container so that the water can be purified at any time.

DIY Aquaponics space

If you plan to create an Aquaponic space inside your house, you will quickly build it yourself. The only items you need are a ready-to-use storage rack made of PVC and garbage. If you plan to develop a vast space, you will look at purchasing an IBC (industrial packaging for liquids) for the garden. It is often a one-cubic-meter, watertight block that is useful for growing a lot of fish. You will make another block above or next to the container with the plants. Add a pump to create a pathway for nutrition. You will be almost able to use your aquaponic location. Confirm that everything is tightened correctly and adjust the correct water temperature to suit the fish you are using.

Aquaponics can be very organic and environmentally friendly for growing vegetables and fish. Even though aquaponics has only been used for a few years, it is an older feature. Because of aquaponics, a person is often self-sufficient, a bit like the people were before the economic revolution. This creates low mass-consumption, another factor why aquaponics is so durable.

CHAPTER 2: NUTRIENT CYCLE

When land organisms consume proteins, they eventually break them down into amino acids then into ammonia. Ammonia (NH_3) is dirty stuff - it is very toxic - and the easiest way to get rid of excess ammonia is to grow it. So, in land animals, ammonia is converted into a urea chemical and excreted in the urine.

In aquaponic systems, nitrogen is uniformly present. It enters the type of fish meal. Fish consume food, but the method is simple; The germs in their vines break down the protein just below ammonia and ammonium. Ammonia is usually present as ammonium (NH_4^+), which travels to fish cell membranes and eventually spreads to water. No additional conversion is required. For the fish, anyway.

Depending on your water's pH, ammonium can remain ammonium or become ammonia, which can be extremely dangerous. There is no charge of ammonia, so it is difficult to keep fish out of its body. When this happens, the fish is poisoned.

Therefore, once ammonia is within the solution, it will have to be replaced or eventually kill the fish. There are two ways to do this: changing your pH in favor of ammonium (which is not suggested) or converting ammonia to nitrate. A series of changes from an organic form (ammonia) to a plant-available form (nitrate) - later stages within the cycle - is called nitrification.

Nitrification

Nitrification is the process that drives most aquaponic systems. Essentially, nitrification converts ammonia and ammonium into useful nitrates. It occurs in two approaches: converting ammonia to nitrite and nitrite to nitrate.

In most environments (except for anaerobic environments), ammonia quickly converts to nitrite (NO_2^-). Microorganisms in soil or solution- or nitrifying bacteria, add oxygen (or oxidation) to ammonia. While this is frequently happening, microbes get the energy to repair carbon (breaking down carbon from CO_2 to form cells). Additionally, hydrogen ions (H^+) are produced - the very ions measured within the pH test, and the water becomes acidic.

This process has traditionally been attributed to a bacterium called Nitrosomonas. Recent research suggests that there are many hundreds, if not thousands, of different species in addition to Nitrosomonas that also work.

The next step within the cycle is to convert that nitrite to nitrate. Nitrite is additionally quite toxic, so you never want to overdose in your system. Fortunately, it represents the energy stored for other [nitrifying] bacteria. These bacteria oxidize nitrite and use power from the method to repair more carbon. Sounds familiar, except for this point, the result of nitrate (NO_3-). Nitrate can be a relatively non-toxic type of nitrogen that can form plants and can be used to make calls.

The bacterium most recognized for carrying out this reaction is named Nitrobacter. Again, however, research indicates that many bacteria participate during this reaction in addition to Nitrobacter.
As bacteria oxidize ammonia and nitrite, they release hydronium ions to the north, making the system more acidic. (For those who want to run their plans within the optimum pH range for nutrient availability, nitrification is the most crucial process for low pH). This means that the answer from older systems tends toward more acidic pH values.

Nitrification efficiency and pH

The speed at which the answer changes; however, it can affect the size of available nitrogen also due to nitrification efficiency. If nitrifying bacteria are not given time to regulate changing pH levels (like almost any other system variable), nitrification will suffer.

Nitrification goodbyes low pH values, as nitrifying ecology, is given time to regularize. Nitrating bacteria are usually inefficient when it changes system variables. They often die or become inactive due to exposure to excessive amounts of light, temperature fluctuations, salinity, and pH fluctuations, as well as many other changes in their environments.

Denitrifying bacteria

The perceived balance between and nitrification efficiency in aquaponics has supported the idea that aquaponic systems' nitrification activity was primarily a function of two distinct groups of bacteria.

In lab tests, these bacterial species have shown sensitivity to pH, with pH changes affecting their ability to oxidize ammonia (Nitrosomonas) and nitrite (Nitrobacter). Remember that most nitrifying bacteria (thus far the least studied) do not handle changing environmental variables well. This is often important to understand for two reasons:

Changing your pH rapidly will reduce your nitrification efficiency.
Most nitrifiers are extremely hard to get rid of from the environment and culture during a laboratory.
Why do I want to understand this?

What does this need to do with the nitrification debate? Well, point # 1 tells us that perhaps many of the reasons for the "system crash" to reduce system pH very well can be attributed to the low system ph.
Point # 2 tells us that Nitrosomonas and Nitrobacter may not be the most critical nitrifiers in the system - they are the most specific group to isolate and grow Petri dishes during the lab.

What does this mean?

This means that the hard and fast rules of nitrification may not be as hard and fast as they usually communicate. Many systems are running in a low pH range with excellent nitrification efficiency (including ours). It is going to be that Nitrosomonas and Nitrobacter species are the first nitrifiers in our system, but the truth is that we do not know. What we know is that our nitrification is not specific to our system ph.

Nitrification in soils

To put this in perspective, there are many acidic soil and marine environments worldwide where nitrification occurs in a low pH range. Many nitrifiers in these environments are not members of nitrobacteria or Nitrosomonas groups. Many of them are unknown. A shovel of soil is an estimated 10,000 different bacteria species or roughly double the number of bacteria currently known to science.

Keeping this in mind, I think this is not just possible, but there are chances that there are some fascinating bacteria that perform nitrifying functions in aquaponic systems worldwide.

In any case, the top product is nitrate (NO3-). Some plants can take ammonium and use it. However, most prefer nitrate. In systems where there is more than ammonium, the plant may be leggier and often less salable. On the other hand, in systems with multiple nitrates, problems with aphids and other pests are often more dramatic, requiring more intervention. So, remember that plans with too many nitrates can see increased issues with pains.

Nitrate, nitrite, and ammonia levels are often easily tested with a freshwater test kit like this. Nitrate dissolves within the slurry and is immediately competed by bacteria, fungi, algae, and other plants. All those organisms are using and using nitrate in their tissues. Because bacteria, fungi, and algae die, nitrogen (often within the protein type) re-enters the system and therefore begins the cycle again.
However, most nitrate, the zone, is transported to the safe and sound-based location, where the plants in your system take it up and use it to grow.

Ideal Nitrate Level

While it is dangerous to keep ammonia or nitrite levels above two ppm and one ppm, respectively, nitrates often run above 100 ppm (well off for many nitrate tests) without posing a threat to your fish. Can. Many hydroponic systems run nitrates within the range of 160 ppm. Plants can often appreciate above that level, but aquaponic producers must balance fish requirements, system ecology (including pests), and, therefore, plant requirements. For this reason, I would like to recommend that most aquaponic growers should shoot permanent, consistent plant growth within the range of 40–80 ppm to take care of their nitrates.

Maintaining a consistent nitrate range

Many systems have difficulty maintaining nitrogen levels, mostly because as the system matures, plants grow more extensive, and therefore, system ecology becomes more complicated. This may need to be fed to meet the increased demand. Many initially want to increase the stocking density, but this is often an error. Instead, increase feeding rates (but do not breastfeed more!), And see if higher nitrate levels are usually achieved with equal amounts of fish.

In addition to fish feed, nitrogen enters the system through fertilizers. Most fertilizers have an NPK rating that tells you the relative concentrations (in that order) of nitrogen, phosphorus, and potassium. For vegetative growth (growth of stems, leaves, and roots), nitrogen requires many other mineral nutrients.

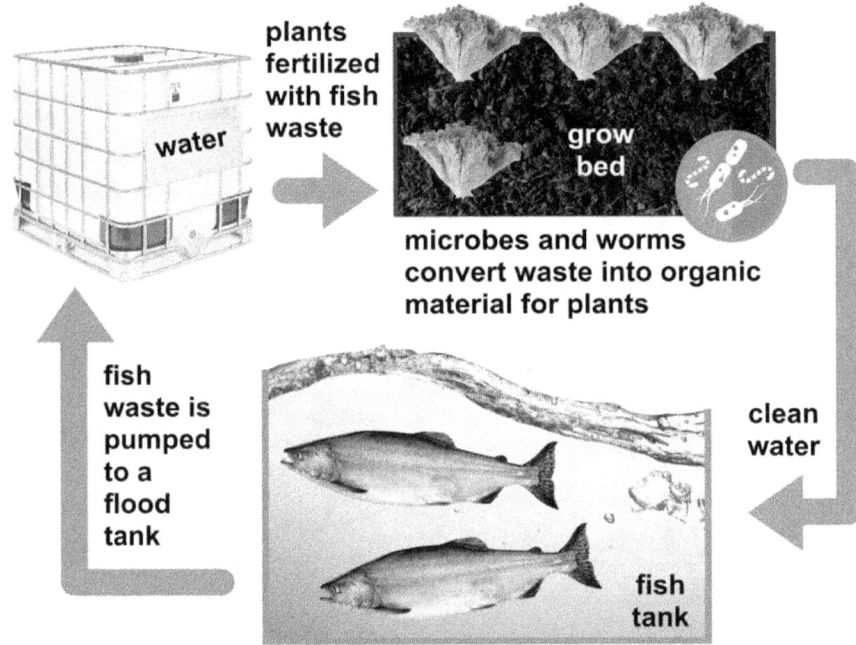

CHAPTER 3: TYPES OF AQUAPONICS SYSTEMS

MEDIA FIDDLE

The bed is a media-based aquaponics system, also known as flood and drain. The most common small-scale aquaponics system is the fashionable do-it-yourself (DIY) backyard home system. Media-based techniques are efficient and straightforward with design space and an initial coffee cost suitable for beginners in aquaponics.

How a media-based Aquaponics system works is media-based growing beds with growing media (expanded soil pebbles, gravels, lava rock) in which vegetables are planted. Water is pumped from the aquarium or flowed into the growing beds by gravity so that plants can access nutrients. The developed media are porous to allow more efficient nutrient uptake of water and prevent solids and other organisms from entering the aquarium to filter the water.

The growing bed is the site for both mineral and biological filters and minerals. Grown beds also host a colony of nitrifying bacteria and supply an area for plants to grow.

Exiting the growing beds, water flows into the sump tank by gravity. Now, the water is clean and released from solids, and then pumped into the aquarium. The water entering the aquarium causes the water level to rise and reach the beds growing back from the aquarium, completing the cycle.

Some media-based aquaponics systems travel by flooding and draining growing beds, employing bell siphons to empty the water when saturation is reached. Once the water reaches a particular level on the rising bed, the bell siphon will drain the rising bed's water. This process will draw oxygen into the growing bed to benefit germs and, therefore, plants. It is an often-endless regular cycle that gives plants all the necessary nutrients to grow without fertilizers.

Other grow-bed irrigation methods use a continuous water flow, either entering one side of the bed and opposite or exiting through a drip irrigation array.

The Filtration

Developed media can act as very efficient filters for mechanical and biological filtration during media-based aquaponics systems. Media-based systems use a mixture of water for plants and filters for plant growing areas. Additionally, it also provides a place to be mineralized. However, high stocking densities can cause heavy mechanical filtration that will clog the media and produce dangerous anaerobic spots.

Mechanical filter

Grow media serves as an external filter, capturing and solid fish waste and other temporary debris. The captured solid wastes will break down over time and become mineralized. A well-balanced media-based aquaponics system will process all solid waste. When the growing bed and growing media are not adequately sized for stocking density, the ever-increasing bed is often filled with solids. To avoid clogging, ensure the stocking density, feeding ratio, and feed rate are in the correct proportions.

Biological filtration is, of all aquaponics methods, biological filtration due to the increasing presence of media in a media-based system on which bacteria can grow. However, if the temperature drops or if the water quality is low, the biofiltration capacity is lost or limited in the event of an increase.

The three areas of the media-based Aquaponics system media-based aquaponics system
are the three growing bed areas within the, and each room has different functions within the system.

Zone 1 - Surface or dry location. This area is within the primary 1- 2 "(5 cm) of the growing bed. This area is named the dry site and acts as a lightweight barrier, allowing sunlight to hit the water directly. It can be prevented, which can lead to the growth of algae. " The zone preclude the expansion of fungi and other harmful bacteria at the bottom of the stem of the plant. Beneficial bacteria are sensitive to direct sunlight, and this area also helps reduce evaporation from beds by covering the wet zone with direct light.

Zone 2 - Base Zone. This is often where plant roots grow and where all plants do an activity. Area 2 is a 4 - 6 "(10-15 cm) area of the growing bed and is an area that is regularly flooded and drained. For

Flooding and exhaust cycles, incoming water is the world's moisture, nutrients, and incoming solids. The fish helps disperse the waste particles. When it is time to flood and drain the cycle, the portions of the drain the water ultimately, this exhaust allows for efficient delivery of oxygen-rich air to the plants' root zone. Gives.

If flooding is not used in exhaust technology, this area is where the water flows through. In this area, the worms are liable to break down the solid waste and which nutrients in the system release the elements.

Zone 3— Solid Collection and Mineral Zone. This is often the last zone, within the last 2 "(5 cm) of the bed growing that is still permanently wet. During this region, small solid waste accumulates, so those active in the mineral are at the forefront. These organisms break down wastes into small fractions and molecules absorbed by the plant through minerals.

Media-based system and drawbacks
- Advantages of relatively cheap and straightforward.
- Plants suitable for all types of plants, from leafy greens to large.
- Minimum cleaning is required.
- Red worms are often added to the gravel bed for a further breakdown of fish waste.
- The media performs a filtering action, preventing debris from returning to the tank.
- Air is present among the particles, supplies— oxygen to the roots.
- Suitable for hobby applications, home gardens, and as a part of commercial farmland.

Disadvantages
- Right quality mediums are often relatively expensive.
- Acne within the SP medium can stop over time, causing anaerobic conditions to worsen for your plants.
- This may require cleaning of the growing bed.
- By itself, this style system is generally not suitable for business purposes for low

productivity and difficulty during large-scale implementation.
- Media beds are bulky and wish for a robust and rigid structure.
- The reduction of media-based aquaponics systems is essential for the farmer to have comfortable content.

- Growth media should have an outer area for bacteria to grow.
- The material should be neutral pH and inert (non-toxic).
- It should have good drainage properties.
- The figure is comfortable with.
- Sufficient space for air and water to flow within the medium.
- Durable and cost-effective.

Aquariums

are an essential component of fish tank aquaponics. Fish need specific conditions to thrive and survive. Therefore, the aquarium should be chosen wisely. There are important aspects that require consideration in choosing your aquarium.

Size

Size of Although any tank will work, round tanks with flat bottles are recommended for aquaponics. A shaped tank allows water to circulate evenly and transfer the solid waste towards the tank's center. Square tanks with flat bottom work but require active, reliable waste removal. Tank sizes affect water circulation and are risky for tanks with poor circulation. Artistically shaped tanks with multiple curves and bends can create outs with dead spa [no circulation within the water.

These areas collect waste and create anoxic conditions hazardous to fish. It is vital to settle on a tank that matches aquatic species' characteristics because many species of downstream fish show better growth and less stress with sufficient horizontal space.

Materials must be either a robust and inert plastic or fiberglass due to their durability and long lifetime. Plastic and fiberglass are easy to apply for plumbing and are exceptionally lightweight. The metal is not appropriate due to corrosion. If you work in plastic containers, confirm that they are food-grade and UV-resistant, as direct sunlight can destroy the plastic.

Color white or other light-colored fish tanks are appropriate because they allow fish to be seen inside the tank. White tanks also reflect daylight and keep the water cool.

Enlarge the bed One of the essential components within the media bed system is the mounting bed. A growing bed is where you grow your plants. Confirm your growing bed:

- It was made of food-grade material that will not leach unwanted chemicals into the water or affect the water's pH.
- Strong enough to carry water and growing media.
- Able to withstand different climates.

- It is often easily connected to other components through simple plumbing parts.
- It is often placed near opposite components.

Size

It can be the standard size rectangle for media beds. Large grow beds are often used, but they require support to lift their weight. However, the growing beds should not be so vast that the farmers/operators cannot reach at least halfway.

Depth and Size

A media-based developed bed should have an appropriate depth and size with the amount of fish present and supply sufficient filtration for nutrient-rich water. The center of the growing bed is essential because it determines which type of vegetables are often grown.

Grow beds should be about 12 inches fully to optimize plant growth and cultivate beneficial ecosystems within the bed. When choosing your grow bed, the rule of thumb is to use a 1: 1 ratio of your grow bed to the aquarium in smaller systems. This suggests that the volume of the growing bed should be sufficient for the importance of the aquarium. This is often not a hard rule but a direct rule to follow when starting.

Develop Media

Many materials are often used as a medium during a base system. However, the press must be organic and have sufficient area to allow bacteria to thrive for water flow to the plant's roots. The medium should have a neutral pH so that water quality is not affected. It is good to rub the media thoroughly before placing it in your grow bed to ensure that there are no dangerous particles that will possibly harm the fish.

Grow Media Options

This is the smallest amount of expensive and most readily available medium yield, gray "gravel is the best for supporting tall plants, and it is not loaded like gravel or short peas. The stone is heavy. Is and as is not liked. Grow small plants because they are often rough on the hands. Another drawback of using stone is that it does not stand efficiently, which can sometimes cause the bacteria needed in your system. It can be difficult to colonize. It is crucial to test vinegar—gravel before placing it in your system, as limestone is usually present within the stone.

Clay pebbles make

LECA (Lightweight Expanded Clay Aggregate) a highly effective growing medium. K is heat-processed clay balls. Clay pebbles are light enough to maneuver. When around easily and heavy plants to supply enough support for low to medium plants. (You need corn like Tall plants may have to support / tie-up, for example) they are also non-degraded, Non-toxic, and pH neutrals. Clay pebbles are expensive compared to contrast mediums, but because it is reusable, lightweight and pH neutral; Clay pebbles are an investment that will last for many years.

Lava rock

Naturally formed lava rock that cools rapidly, which does not give the airtime to escape, effectively trapping it. This trapped air creates a highly porous surface, enhancing the rock world and creating many openings for nitrifying bacteria to measure. Lava rock is lightweight and features a neutral pH, so it will not affect your system's balance. Lava rocks are often sharp; however, you want to use them with caution.

Bell siphon

A bell siphon, also known as an auto-siphon, can be a robot that wants to regulate water flow quickly and efficiently in an aquaponic system. The water from the siphon spontaneously developed bed is drained into the aquarium. The water is then grown from the aquarium. The siphon also maintains a minimum water level and drains out any excess water.

The best plant to grow media-based aquaponics systems is the demand for different nutrients in vegetables. In aquaponics, plants are classified to support their nutrient demand.

Plants with low nutrient demand include leafy greens and herbs such as lettuce, basil, peppermint, chives, parsley, coriander, Choy, hyacinth, peas legumes. Plants with moderate nutrient demand are cabbage, bananas, cauliflower, broccoli, onions, carrots, and taro.
Plants with high nutrient demand, also known as nutrient hungry plants, are tomatoes, brinjals, cucumbers, strawberries, and peppers.

NUTRIENT FILM TECHNIQUES

Nutrient Film Technique (NFT) is a hydroponic growing technique yet effective design that works well in some environments because of its simplicity and can be adapted to aquaponics. This method uses horizontal pipes (usually PVC pipes) that have shallow streams of nutrient-rich water. The plants are planted within holes at the top of the line and are ready to use this thin film of nutrient-rich water.

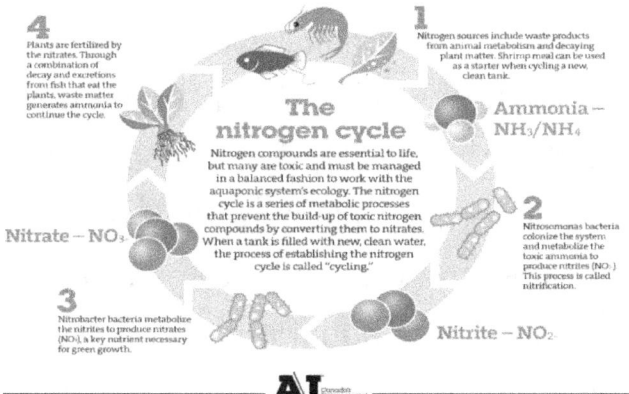

The nutrient film technique system is mainly used in the cultivation of greens with small root systems. NXT is popular for commercial aquaponics because it is more feasible than opposite aquaponics methods. This system is additionally more useful in urban areas where space and food production are considerations. However, it is costly to line up at such locations and is not suitable when suppliers do not have sufficient access.

What a nutrient film technology works in NXT, water is pumped or flows through mechanical filters and by gravity in the filter or sump tank. Some water is pumped directly from the sump tank into the aquarium, while the remaining water is pumped and evenly distributed through the NXT pipe. The water then flows down again through the growing pipes where the saplings are planted. Upon exiting the ever-increasing lines, the water is returned to the filter or sump and then to the aquarium or the cables. Water entering the aquarium flows through the pipe exiting the tank and goes back to the mechanical filter, completing the cycle.

Unlike the media-based system, the nutrient film technique does not require a flood period because the water in the NFT flows continuously from the aquarium. The growing pipe has several holes at the highest line where the plants are placed and grow. After the plants start consuming nutrient-rich water, the growers will start developing root systems inside the tube. The shallow film of water at the bottom of each line ensures that the roots receive an external oxygen amount.

In NFTA mechanical and Biological Filtration In an NXT system, mechanical and biological filtration is critical because it does not have sufficient area to supply bacteria habitat. This often occurs because mechanical and biological filters are constructed to act as a physical trap to capture solid waste and natural filters for nitrification.

A biofilter is usually a tank or barrel that holds a porous medium that is aerated heavily and will be located after the aquarium and solid filter before returning to the water plant channels.

Water travels through the aquarium → solid filter → biofilter → NXT channel → aquarium.

NXT Grow Pipes Following the Above mentioned filtration methods, NXT uses plastic pipes (usually PVC pipes) that are done horizontally to grow plants using water within the aquaponics system. Lines are often arranged in multiple patterns and may use vertical space, walls, fences, and overhanging balconies.

Water is pumped from the biofilter into each pipe with a uniformly uniform flow, creating a stream of shallow nutrient-rich water flowing under the rock. As plants consume nutrient-rich water from the stream, they grow a root inside the growing pipe. Maintaining a shallow stream of water ensures that the bases receive large amounts of oxygen in the root zone.

The size and shape of the pipe.

Increase of the Next, pipes with a square cross-section are the best, but most aquaponics farmers use round tubes because it is readily available in most locations. It is advisable to settle on a line with the optimum diameter for the type of plant. Large fruiting plants, use 11 cm diameter growing pipes, while for small root mass with fast-growing leafy greens and small vegetables, use lines growing 7.5 cm in diameter.

Grow Pipes Within planting holes are drilled into the mounting pipes (7–9 cm diameter), and the use of these holes must match the dimensions of the Internet cup. Each plant should have a minimum of 21 cm in the middle to allow sufficient plant space. The seeding is placed during a plastic net cup and then placed within the mounting pipe hole. Internet cups will support plants. An area of about 8 inches between each plant has been suggested to allow sufficient plant space for the plants. Media such as clay pebbles or gravels are often placed for planting within pure cups to balance and support the plants.

Weaknesses of power and NFT

Roots exposed in a share will receive several breaths of air as the basis to help prevent plant disease.

The constant flow of water - The continuous flow of water within the system helps prevent the build-up of solids at the roots and ensures that nutrient-rich water is generally available to the plant, increasing their growth and health.

Constant flow reduces fungal risk - Constant agitation of water helps reduce the risk of fungal growth.

Weaknesses

Can block root channels - underwater swinging plants are perfect for plant health. However, because plants grow, large roots can block channels, preventing water from moving into the plant's remaining parts, which can cause nutrient deficiencies for the plants.

Water temperature fluctuations - Water pumped through channels can quickly cool down or heat up. This often occurs because the water film moving through the NXT channels is extremely thin, subjecting it to temperature fluctuations.

Pump failure can destroy the yield - if the pump fails, the plants may not have access to water and may rapidly wilt or die.

Only little plants can grow — heat greens and small vegetable plants are best, but large plants with extensive root systems are not compatible with NXT.

DEEP WATER COLTURE

Deepwater Culture or DWC can be a modern variant of aquaponics, the oldest type of hydroponics, or aquaponics. DWC systems are found in the same way that ancient civilizations are like Aztecs, and so the earliest Asian cultures evolved. Not only have they proved useful with this long history, but trouble culture also provides many benefits.

This type of aquaponics setup is reasonably low maintenance, perfect for fast-growing plants such as lettuce and leafy greens, and can be quickly grown to almost any size. Understanding what a troubled culture system means, what the essential components are, and some suggestions will thank you for being one of the most comfortable and most effective types of aquaponic systems.

The trouble culture system

DOC setup shares similarities with other specialized aquaponics systems, including the need for regular monitoring to ensure fish, plants, and bacteria's health. Cycling is necessary when starting a perturbation culture system to determine a bacterial colony. Although it shares these similarities, Trouble Culture Aquaponics has many differences from other setups. During such a scenario, the plant roots become submerged or remain submerged most of the time. There is no water to extract water from the growing beds, and additional nutrients are added to the circulation of water rather than to water flow and flooding. In many cases, a developed media is unnecessary, although your system is often designed to use lightweight media. Pure pots are more fashionable DWC, providing stability to plants without a more developed medium.

Two primary types of trouble culture are often employed, although many design variations you use. The most common options are those that float on top of a tank and those using the canal system. The only variant is the tank float variety. It requires the lowest total components and can be used with natural water sources such as ponds, indoor or outdoor tanks, and even aquariums. In this system, there are floating grow beds above the fish's habitat and some means of aeration. A canal system is only slightly more complicated. With this style, the aquarium is separated from the floating grow bed, and water from the aquarium is pumped into one or more canals, where the plant sheet climbs. This method is somewhat better, in that water is circulated more efficiently.

Even though DWC is in your favor, all trouble systems use some or most of the later essential components:
- **Aquariums** - Fish habitats are often as large or as small as you favor. It is often the holding tank for the bulk of the water within the system and is home to fish. It also functions because the collection reservoir for fish waste is

- **Biofilter** - the home of the biofertilizer nitrification process. This is often the case where beneficial bacteria turn fish waste into plants into usable, nutrient-rich food.
- **Filters** - It is often used to capture solid waste, materials, and anything that can find its way into the system. Vortex filters or other filter methods, including screen or reverse osmosis filters, can also be used.
- **Pump** - During a canal system, pumps are employed to filter water from the aquarium and force it into the canals. Pumps are also used to reproduce troublesome culture systems. This keeps the water flowing. The dimensions and strength of the pump will depend on the dimensions of the tank.
- **Aeration method** - In any system, it is crucial to add more oxygen to the water. Dissolved oxygen is essential for the health and growth of both fish and, therefore, plants. Air pumps, diffusers, air stones, or other methods may be used.
- **Canals** - In canal systems, canals are pipes or furrows that seek to capture water pumped from the aquarium and therefore grow beds for plants. Multiple troughs are often added to the system, allowing more room for plant expansion.

- **Floating Grow Bed -** This is often habitat for plants. Floating beds are usually constructed from foam or a light material with foam. Plants are placed in holes within the bed, causing their roots to fall into the water. Pure pots are often employed for added stability and to prevent plants from falling.

Deepwater culture tips

With some simple tips, trouble culture aquaponics, are often highly productive. First, remember that aeration is essential. Water needs either air added with pumps or air stones or some method to increase dissolved oxygen content. This can be maintained daily to ensure that your plants and fish have too much oxygen to enhance their growth. Additionally, test your water regularly to verify the pH level. Within a suitable range, the water temperature remains constant, and therefore the nitrification process is operating at an optimal level. If you are employing a canal or rearranging the trouble culture system, regularly check the pumps and any piping for the correct function and remove any material from the filter that may cause a clause or blockage. Finally, may end in use plants and fishes that are easy to worry about, overgrow, and are disease resistant. This can ensure maximum yield from your system.

VERTICAL TOWERS

Vertical aquaponics simply refers to an aquaponics system that goes upwards. This will increase the amount of space you get without the need for more floor space. This will be an attractive option once you have a little room in or outside your home.

A simplified version of vertical aquaponics is the standard IBC tort set, Where the developed bed lies at the top of the aquarium. But it is often just one layer; an existing vertical system will specialize in growing more and more plants on top of every other.

The trick to a successful vertical aquaponics system is to ensure that every plant has enough room for growing and adequate lighting, Reducing spacing between plants. The advantage of vertical towers is that you can simply grow crops effectively one above the other. This enables a 5 ft tall vertical aquaponics tower to maintain plants like the hydroponics system that is up to 10 ft 6 ft but only operated on one level.

The Why vertical aquaponics is so successful is principle of using tubing to create many small pockets where plants can grow. The most common tubing is PVC, so vertical aquaponics is commonly referred to as PVC aquaponics (is food edible-safe?). Your vegetables or other crops are grown without soil. Vertical gardens are usually built above the fish tank to keep the system as simple as possible.

Your fish must be fed, and therefore, water temperature, pH, nitrates, and ammonia levels are monitored. A small pump will then take water filled with nutrients and release it into the highest cylindrical tubes that form the vertical aquaponics tower. The water glides within the PVC aquaponics pipe and provides its nutrients to your plants.

Air will flow through the pipes that provide the plants with oxygen that reaches the roots through the leaves. The air will rotate the tubes because the water will not fill the boxes.

If your aquaponics towers are functioning correctly, the plants will clean the water before returning the fish; Your fish and plants will interfere with you the least.

The system is essentially self-contained, although you will occasionally have to add a touch of water.

However, it is essential to note that the PVC vertical aquaponics system described below will filter. Before the plants can be carried water. The justification is just to get rid of any solid waste. If you do not, the trash will attach to the plants' roots and prevent them from getting nutrients.

If you are employing a conventional system with growing beds, the bacteria will remove all waste products, but this does not often occur during a PVC vertical aquaponics system.

How to create your vertical aquaponics system is not difficult; You all want to follow these steps, then you will begin to bear the fruits of your labor.

You will need:

- 4-inch diameter pipes; about 20 feet
- Elbows4 inches in diameter:4 and 6
- T connectors between inches: 4 to 6
- 100-gallon containers
- between Aquarium tubing -of about 20 feet - for
- 4-way splitters1-inch pipes.
- plastic cups
- Scrap Fabric
- electrical tape
- aquarium pump capable of transferring 400 gallons per hour
- filters

It is worth noting that almost any fish is often used in such a system. However, if this is usually your first aquaponics vertical tower system, you can settle on tilapia; Providing its local climate allows this. They are generally extraordinarily adventurous and cheap.

In terms of plants, the most straightforward options are leafy vegetables, herbs, and even tomatoes (although these are generally better when you have a mature system because they demand high levels of nutrients, Huh).

These will not take up so much space that the opposite plants do not get light, but they will give you a big crop so that you can get an honest crop. If you want to increase the spread of plants, then they also complement each other.

Step 1 - Pipe Work

The exact amount of 4-inch pipe you employ will determine how large your completed aquaponics towers are or what percentage of them you have gained.

A good starting line is to make eight one-foot-long pieces. In six of those pieces, you will use one hole to make two holes; evenly spaced.

You can then drill a 1-inch hole into one of the foot-long pieces that have not already found a circular hole. This is often where the water will return to the aquarium.

Step 2 - Putting the Pipes Together

Now lay your pipes in the following order. One 90 ° piece, 1 feet piece, one T junction, 1 feet piece, T junction, 1 feet piece, and 90 ° bit.

Do this again, and you should be ready to use two additional and feet pieces (1 with drainage holes) to tie the entire lot together within the shape of a rectangle.

Electrical tapes or similar tapes are often not used to join these pieces together. All T junctions are confirmed similarly; Upwards. The holes within the pipe must also be upward except for drain holes that must meet within the rectangle.

Step 3-Upstream Pipes

This is where you are getting growing space and room together with your DIY vertical aquaponics system.

Cut four pieces of 4-inch diameter pipe. They should be 2 to three feet tall; You are installing your vertical aquaponics system; in which ratio you must count the height there.

These pipes will turn into tee junctions like the four chimneys in your PVC aquaponics universe.

But before you can do this, you need to add the holes found in your DIY vertical aquaponics. You want to use your 1-inch hole to drill five spots on the side of your pipe; Confirm that they are evenly spaced. Rotate the pipe 90 ° and drill another four holes; The peak should sit between the holes you have just prepared. Keep the pipe on, and repeating it, make four holes in 5 holes until you have covered the entire line alternately in the spot.

Now repeat it with the opposite three vertical aquaponics pipes. These are the largest mounting holes. As you will appreciate, there are likely to be 18 to 25 holes in each of your lines. Each of those holes represents a plant; There are more than 100 plants in 4 tubes.

Step 4 - Position your vertical aquaponics system. Your vertical aquaponics system.

Now it is time to decide where to go to take a seat. If you have used the IBC Tote, it will have already received a frame. You would prefer to use an optional container or perhaps two 50-gallon drums.

Whatever you have decided to live in your fish, confirm that they are food grade containers, which you have previously given them an honest wash.

Then place them in their required location and confirm that they are well supported if necessary.

It is crucial to think about your access to the fish tank; If you see a problem, you will have to check your fish, feed them, or perhaps remove them.

It is also important to hide the aquarium with a dark material or perhaps paint it. This can prevent daylight from going into the water, which can cause your vertical aquaponics system to develop and damage the balance.

Step 5 - Add Vertical Garden

You will now have to place a PVC aquaponics vertical tower on top of your chosen aquarium. It is vital to ensure that the planting pipe's weight is distributed throughout your tank; Excessive weight gain at one location can offer you issues as the plant grows.

If the system is outside, you should also consider the wind factor; Pipes are relatively light, you do not want them to blow; it will be necessary to plan their systems to hustle them into the situation.

Now is also a real-time to cut a small section of the aquarium pipe into the one-inch drain hole you created earlier.

The aquarium pipe should be left downstream, minimizing any issues with the flow of water.

It is necessary to note that a small angle on your PVC towers will ensure all the water flow where the drainage holes are; Making sure it returns to the tank.

Step 6 - Add Cups

Vertical holes should not require cups, but if you do not put them horizontally, your plants will either be washed out of the way, or their roots will block the pipes.

To help prevent this, you will want to spread half a dozen holes under the rock of plastic cups and then drop them into horizontal holes.

Step 7 - Grow the media.

Plants found something to grow in, and they are ready to be fed for nutrients within the water. To try to do this, you will need to get some Rockwool or some pond filter foam. This is often perfect for working in the holes you cut within vertical tubes. Your seeds are often pushed into this foam. Otherwise, you may pierce them a bit to keep them inside.

It is a simple idea to place burlap sacks or similar material inside your vertical tubes before inserting them into the pipe. It can absorb water; Pipe, and back into the aquarium by slowing its flow.

In this process, slow water is often absorbed by saliva, and so seeds or small plants may receive the nutrients they have to grow.

Burlap will give something to lock the roots; This can protect each plant in its position and help prevent seeds from blocking the pipe.

Step 8 - Pump

You must have an honest quality pump; It is more expendable to take a touch in a situation that presents a good reputation such that fish and plants can die if it breaks.

As already mentioned, the pump needs to pump 400 gallons of water per hour; This can ensure that the water remains aerated, and hence the cycling of the water is done. However, you will need a more powerful pump if your vertical aquaponics system is exceptionally high.

The pump is located within the aquarium. Ideally, it should be raised above the rock bottom so that the fish are ready to swim without getting trapped. Read on how to choose the most straightforward pump here.

You must attach several of your aquarium tubings to the pump; The adapter must be equipped with a pump for 1-inch tubing.

It may then be indifferent to the highest part of your vertical column. Here you must split the pipe through a series of adapters so that the water reaches the most elevated of each column. If possible, a 4-way splitter is best to ensure that the water flow is also for all or any vertical column.

If this is often impossible, you will divide it in two, then all sides again in two; Even to maintain the flow.

Now, it is a simple idea to pour some water into your tank and test the system. You do not want to splash water from side to side due to a dirty joint.

Top Tip: It is a simple idea to pre-slide the pipes to heat them on one joint; This can help them travel easily and lock in place.

It is essential to say that if you have opted for two 50-gallon barrels, you must have a pump located in the barrel and, therefore, the return drain going in reverse. You also must make sure that the 2 barrels are interconnected with your pipes so that that water can flow into your vertical aquaponics system.

The best thanks for doing this is to row a pipe within the return barrel adequately. The fish will always have enough water during this barrel; Subsequently, the barrel feeds into the barrel whenever it starts to fall.

Step 9 - Fish and plants

You are now able to add your water too. Let it settle before adding fish to the water. This is often the case, which takes the longest time because you want to get water dechlorinated, taking several days.

You must check the pH level, ammonia, nitrate, and even temperature before adding fish.

It is best to feature some small fish first to help raise ammonia levels and for plants to show up in nitrates to encourage the arrival of bacteria.

DUTCH BUCKETS

BUCKETS Aquaponics can be a great way to grow plants faster and more efficiently than more traditional methods. The very fact that you can breed fish just at the same time can be a big bonus.
However, growing plants with nutrients provided by fish is not new; Dating back to Aztec is proof of practice!

It is a little surprising that there are many different approaches, all of which have their properties. The Dutch Bucket Aquaponics system is worth talking about because it is straightforward and surprisingly effective.

What is a Dutch Bucket Aquaponics System?
In short, the Dutch Bucket Aquaponics system uses buckets attached to your aquarium. You will have several bucket serials, all connected to the aquarium via a central line. Water is pumped through it and into each bucket; The aquarium is then allowed to empty again.

The option is to pump water into your bucket during a continuous flow; Effectively keeping the roots submerged. For this to be effective, you must confirm that the water is well aerated. This system does not use tones.

The bucket is loaded with your growing media. Ideally, you will have a lid with a large hole from which your plant can move out. You will also put some dry media on top to prevent algae growth.

Water grows through the media, allowing bacteria to convert ammonia into nitrates and provide nutrition to plants. It collects within the lowest inch or two before leaving its way into the aquarium.

Aside from the fact that a simple system to determine, the Dutch bucket aquaponics system is fantastic for ensuring your plant roots do not interfere with your system. Applying only one thing to each container makes it easy to incorporate these roots. This makes it especially good for large plants, such as fruit trees or those who want to climb like tomatoes.

The constant supply of nutrients allows plants to grow naturally in less space.

With this, the Dutch bucket aquaponics method avoids water loss through evaporation; It is very economical to operate, although you live in a hot climate.

Dutch Bucket System Pros and Cons

There are the pluses and minuses of adopting the Dutch bucket aquaponics system:

Pros

You can add or remove plants very easily; This makes it easier to reduce disease or adapt to your fish and nitrifying bacteria.
Little or no use of water.
Cheap yet effective, most supplies are often sour.

Consistency of roots within the media with a continuous water drip through the drip system increases the likelihood of growth of algae and fungi on your plant's roots.

Despite being easily prepared to remove plants from the group, diseases can spread rapidly and affect all their plants before they have time to react; Especially if they are kept during a greenhouse or similar environment.

You must focus on the temperature of your growing media within the summer. The thermal mass count will vary depending on which media you choose to grow. The heat is hot; your water will be formed; You must add cooling measures. But the heat in the dark will slowly decrease and, combined with your cooling measures, will likely recreate the device.

Best Plants for a Dutch Bucket System One for the pa Dutch Bucket System

It is best to settle on your better plant. A tomato is a prevalent option, but beans, peppers, and eggplants are all excellent choices.

You will also find that it is often a sound system for growing small trees, the bucket preventing roots that limit growth; But you will still have high-quality fruits. Indeed, I can grow faster than growing in soil.

How to Build a Dutch Bucket Aquaponics System
There are a

few ways during which you will build a Dutch bucket system, but the simplest one, especially if this is your first time, is that the following:

Step 1 - Get yourself as much Get the bucket as you think. You must start your system. Place them on a raised bench or stand; Making sure they are above your aquarium.

Step 2 - On the verge of rock bottom, drill a hole within each bucket. You must presently attach a pipe. The pipe most commonly connects to the line, which connects to the exhaust of all buckets. It can be angled downward so that water can flow back into your aquarium.

Step 3- Keep your aquarium so that the water flows into it. Then add a pump to get the water you need from the aquarium and above the bucket. There will be a little pipe coming into this main pipe just above each line. A short tube will allow water to drip from the roots of your plants.

Step 4 - Adding a filter before pumping it into the bucket. At a minimum, it can remove solid waste. You also want an additional biofertilizer facility to help plants get nitrates.

Step 5 - Test your system to ensure that the water seeps easily. You must fill each bucket with an acceptable growing medium but do not add plants yet.

Step 6 - Test the system to ensure that your nitrifying bacteria have settled, and then start adding fish and plants.

Step 7 - Enjoy watching your plants grow.

DTF (DEEP FLOW TECHNIQUE)

Deep flow technique can be a type of NFT technique, which is additionally called Nutrient Flow technique. Instead of thin nutrient film, plants are surrounded by about 4 cm of high nutrient solution. The process required is the same. The system is recirculating.

Deep flow techniques make such hydroponic systems safe, as the roots are still supplied in a pump failure. However, the strategy is often not applicable, especially in tall/large systems, with oxygen availability to plants leading to uneven plant growth.

WICKING BEDS ON BED LICKING

Have you ever heard of aquaponics? Perhaps you recognize the term but are not sure what it means. The big news is that you are close to finding out! Observe this guide to urge everything you would like to understand about bed aquaponics and how to get started.

Everyone should try aquaponics at least once in their life. There is deep satisfaction in growing your food; Especially when it is this easy! More importantly, there are many ways to realize the most specific possible outcomes; you will want to do as many of them as possible.

The original premise behind the wicking beds was to supply a sustainable growing environment in desert conditions.

You cannot sleep in a desert, but this approach will ensure that your plants need water and nutrition, suggesting that you find it easy to grow anything and grow successfully.

What is a wicking bed?

The original venting bed uses rainwater but hooking it into your aquaponics system will not only water your plants, but they will also have nitrates. Chat bedding has generally been described as the best way to grow root vegetables, like carrots and potatoes.

Aquaponics is as close to the warts bed as you would to aquaponics with mud! The wicking bed will have approximately 3" of wicking material to be effective. The fibers often absorb the water and allow it to maneuver upward to the soil that you simply lay on top of it.

There are several different options that you will choose for licking ingredients:

Straw - good at absorbing water but decomposing surprisingly quickly.
Vermiculite - is amazingly useful in creating water reserves as there are many pockets to take a seat in the water, but it can retain moisture, thus preventing plants from moving.

Coco coir - This is often an excellent choice for many plants, such as garlic and onions. It represents a fair balance between water retention, soil support, and aeration.

The real advantage of this technique within the desert is that water cannot evaporate as it is below the soil line; Even within the vats and waiters, your plants will thrive!

Water is pumped from your aquarium to the bottom of this technique. This is usually done once a week; Penetration by a pipe at the highest of the mounting bed prevents soil and other contaminants from entering the warts area.

Licking beds can be an excellent way to expand your growing area without increasing your aquarium's dimensions.

This will allow you to grow virtually any plant and experiment with different techniques to do the best job for you and your environment. But, better of all, the inconsistent fact is that it is often much more comfortable to line up and enhance your current Aquatic system.

Bed wick

Advantages and drawbacks Like any system, there are many advantages and disadvantages:

Pros

You are to the dimensions of your wicking bed the only limit the amount of differentiation you will spare from your aquarium.

Ease of fixing wicking beds, you can use virtually any container to make a venting bed, and then you can have a pipe for water, overflow drain, wicking material, and soil if you wish. This is easy!

Water

harvesting uses a maximum amount of 50% less water than a standard approach for growing plants.

Weed control

because these plants are watered under the highest layer of soil to stay dry. This makes it harder for weeds to determine themselves.

Deficient maintenance

Once you install the system, you put it in water; once a week should be enough. When you are ready, of course, you must cut your plants.

Cons

Location

Aquaponics warts beds should plan any standard aquaponics mounting container; This enables bacteria to convert ammonia into nitrate. If this is not possible, you will need a biofilter in your system before sitting in bed.

Water use

Water is extracted from the aquaponics system for wiping beds, which should not be returned to the aquarium. This suggests that you must change the water in your aquaponics system and confirm that it is the appropriate temperature, pH, etc., for your fish.

Costs

There is no need to spend much to build a wicking bed, especially if you make your day wicking bed. However, it should be noted that this would be quite a standard raised bed expense.

Moisture

You want the soil to remain moist for the plants to urge the necessary nutrients. But, if it is holding its water well, you will find that some vegetables do not grow as well as possible; For more information, see the section on simple plants below.

How to Make A Winter Bed for Aquaponics?

It is surprisingly easy to make a DIY waxing bed, just follow these steps Instructions:

Grab a container

You can use almost anything for it! An old rigid pond liner, bath, or perhaps a refrigerator. Of course, you will just buy a fiberglass tub if you favor it.

There is no set depth you want to keep, but you should keep in mind that all you need is 3 inches of wicking material before entering the soil. Your soil's depth will depend on which plants you want to grow and how deep they want to grow their roots. Ideally, you want to put 6-8 inches of soil above your wart material.

Setting up the system found a container in which you would need to put two pipes. One must be from the bottom of the box and stretch above the container's top; This is often to get back into the water. You will have to drill holes in the bottom of this pipe; Permitting water to fill the warts area.

You can add a 90 ° bend during this pipe and run it under your container's rock, allowing water to flow evenly into the reservoir. Of course, it will also have holes to drain the water out.

This pipe's diameter must match your pump's tube; This can reduce the risk of flow issues or leakage.

Other pipes should be positioned at the opposite end of the licking bed. It should extend from the top of the container to the top and have holes within the bottom (this time let in the water). However, it also needs a 'T' junction with the current pipe; This enables excess water to flow to your system; To prevent soil from becoming flooded.

The T 'junction should be positioned at an equal height as the top of your wicking material.

Top Tip: If you want a simple thank you for tracking the water level, add a transparent window to the side of your container, covering 3-4 under the rock. You must use silicone to ensure that water does not leak from the window.

It is worth noting that the second pipe goes above the container's crest to supply you with additional viewing options. This can help ensure that you have got the water level right.

Bed Preparation

Now you can place your chosen wicking material within the base of your container. It should be uniformly 3" deep and canopy the entire box.

You can place soil directly on top of it, but a layer of weed control fabric is better. This can prevent roots from moving into the wicker bed and damage the water flow.

In this situation, you will be ready to add your soil to your required height; 6"-12" is sufficient for many plants.

Test before planting

Now it is a simple idea to run your pump and fill the wicking area. You do not need to use your aquarium's water to test the system. This will tell you that the pump should be running for a long time and ensure the mud does not start floating. You will know that the waste bed becomes full when the water starts coming out of the overflow pipe.

Once you are proud of it and thoroughly moisten the soil within the process, you will be ready to add your plants.

Aquaponics that just leaves the question of which plants you want to specialize in during the wicking bed aquaponics system?

Wicking bed aquaponics systems are perfect for growing root crops or tuber types. These include potatoes, beets, carrots, lettuce, and most other vegetables. It can be described as the main objective for the work of cleaning a bed in aquaponics.

However, they are not a natural alternative to trees and other perennials that possess deep root structures.

CHAPTER 4: THE BENEFITS OF AQUAPONICS

Why Aquaponics the Organic Aquaponics

Is Better than Bottom Line of There is no cheating on this because we cannot use any kind of chemical pesticides or our fish will die, period.

Even the most approved biological insecticide will kill our fish. The fish acts because "the canary within the coal mine," and aquaponics forces the farmer to be honest. Even our water in the bend contains chlorine, an additive like chlorine that can kill our fish.

Aquaponics mimics the natural symbiotic relationship between fish and plants.

Even traditional organic farms got to supplement their soil with fertilizers. These fertilizers are often inadequate for the health of soils and watersheds.

We are located right next to the city of Bend. You will come to us and see how we grow
our plants and fishes and treat them to ensure that your food is 100% chemical free!

No GMO We do not grow any GMO plants.

Another advantage of growing indoors is that we do not have to worry about the spray from the air flowing fields on our crops. Or mysterious GMO plants appear in our crops like what happened in eastern Oregon.

AQUAPONICS Other Benefits

- Our proprietary system grows six times more per square foot than traditional farming.
- Aquaponics uses 90% less water than traditional farming.
- With our system, we will grow anywhere on Earth, at any time of the year, in any season.
- Because aquaponics recirculates water within the system, we will grow in drought and areas with little water.
- When we are growing indoors, fewer pests are affected.
- There is no weeding!
- Grows twice as fast as plants! Thanks to the naturally frozen water from the fish.

➢ For the commercial farmer, aquaponics produces two streams of income, fish and veggies, rather than just one.
➢ Our aquaculture farm does not require a farm with fertile soil or land with soil; Aquaponics are also often successfully carried out on the sand, gravel, or rocky surfaces, which can never be used as a traditional farm.
➢ Because we hang our growing light vertically and use each side of the sun (no reflectors), our lights are twice as efficient as extending in one area versus two areas of plants.

Environmental water conservation:
Aquaponics uses 90% less water than traditional farming. Water and nutrients are recycled during a closed-loop fashion that conserves water.
Aquaponics protects our rivers and lakes: no harmful fertilizer survives in the water area. In efforts to take care of nutrient-rich soils, farms need to use tons of fertilizers. The additional fertilizer eventually creates in rivers, where there are countless harmful side effects.

Gas Conservation: "Food Miles" is significantly reduced. Our produce travels only five miles from agriculture to the consumer. Only by serving the area do people reduce harmful gas emissions.

Energy conservation: With increasing light, we use less energy than traditional commercial farming! All the life used in aquaponics is electric, so alternative energy systems such as solar, wind, and hydroelectricity are often used to power this farm.

Land Conservation: Our system grows six times more per square foot than traditional farming. Furthermore, by growing in abandoned warehouses, we use structures that already exist, saving money, energy, and other valuable resources.

Health and Nutrition

Our fertilizer comes from cold-blooded fish, unlike fertilizers from warm-blooded animals. Do not take cold or salmonella. Read more here.

Fish is the fastest indicator from plant protein to animal protein.

Fish has no growth hormone, no mercury, no antibiotics, no PCBs (what is PCBS?)

There are no antibiotics in our plants.

It tastes better than those purchased at the grocery (as it is not shipped and stored for extended periods).

Compared to hydroponics

You must continually change your water system, as the nutrient solution makes salts and chemicals within the water. Not only is it wasting more water than aquaponics, but it is also polluting the watershed.

Nutritional solutions for hydro are super expensive, where fish in aquaponics are often fed insects, insects, and scraps from plants.

Hydro rotates in a sterile environment, where aquaponics embraces all microbes as they play an essential role within each growing process. Internally aquaponics possesses fewer diseases and pest problems.

In hydroponics, you do not get to promote and harvest fish.

Hydroponic producers can use toxic chemicals to control pests.

CHAPTER 5: ENVIRONMENTAL IMPACT

1. Water Conservation: Aquaponics uses 90% less water than traditional farming. Water and nutrients are recycled during a closed-loop fashion that conserves water.

2. Aquaponics protects our rivers and lakes: No harmful fertilizer goes into the water area. In efforts to take care of nutrient-rich soils, farms need to use tons of fertilizers. The additional fertilizer eventually creates in rivers, where there are countless harmful side effects.

3. Gas Conservation: "Food Miles" is significantly reduced. Our produce travels only five miles from agriculture to the consumer. Only by serving the area do people reduce harmful gas emissions.

4. Energy conservation: Even with growing lights, we use less energy than traditional commercial farming! All the life used in aquaponics is electric, so alternative energy systems such as solar, wind, and hydroelectricity are often used to power this farm.

5. Land Conservation: Our system grows six times more per square foot than traditional farming.

6. Resourceful: By growing abandoned warehouses, we use structures that already exist, saving money, energy, and other valuable resources.

CHAPTER 6: BIOLOGICAL SURFACE AREA

The Region is the soul of an exemplary system. Aquaponic producers have several of the most critical innovative people globally; They have used almost everything as a growing media! From river rock, expanded clay, expanded ore (perlite), naturally sour peat or coco coir, and even materials such as packing of popcorn. Producers have found ways to grow within exceptionally low probability aquaponic media.

We have been using various media for years and have a couple of our favorites. Before I tell you what our choice is, you know about the overall odds, tradeoffs, and media types' benefits.

Different aquaponic media have additional benefits and challenges. Commercial producers, especially those, must remember that they will plan costs accordingly.

Although the pros and cons may include traits such as cost, convenience, weight, water movement, plant anchoring, and more, there is a symptom that seems to regulate many of these areas.

Most symptoms and functions are either directly or indirectly associated with the. The
area surface area is integral to the engines of the aquaponic system - the microbes - which profoundly affect other functions. Two things directly suffer from the amount of area.

Nutrient cycling is the conversion of ammonia into nitrates and is essential for health. Nitrifying bacteria drive cycling. The region serves as a habitat for those bacteria and may be causally linked to the system's speed and amount of nutrient rotation.

When it is hosting germs, the region is named Biological Zone, or BSA. The BSA is one of the direct benefits of a higher sector. With high BSA, the system gets better at disturbances, keeps the pH better, and responds to faster feeding.

Another direct benefit to the region is the cation exchange capacity (CEC). CEC is the ability of media particles to carry interchangeable citations. (Atoms in the cation are charged during a solution.) Since many nutrients are required, the salts in crops that dissolve in water, the nutrient hold for many nutrients is equal.

Good CECs mean low fluctuations in nutrient levels. It can also provide a buffer against acidification. This prevents the pH from drying out quickly.

The surface area also indirectly affects the aquatic system. The site has an inverse relation to particle size; the larger the particle, the lower the area. The smaller the particle, the more remarkable space.

The problem is that both larger particles and smaller particles have advantages and challenges.

Larger particles like hydroelectricity are more comfortable maneuvering, and it is easier to stay with plants, remain clean, and have water movement. The pore space between the particles is so large that solids rarely gather and cause blockages or anaerobic areas.

Smaller particles provide much higher BSA and CEC but are often difficult to detect. The small pore space means that solid can accumulate, which may cause anaerobic decomposition. Sometimes even tiny particles can become compressed. This introduces a new set of issues with planting and maintenance.

Because each particle size's advantages are playing on different sides, producers may not get all the advantages of an aquaponic media type. They need to select and choose the benefits that they get.
Fibers ignore the traditional field trade.
Fibers turn on particle size and the competitive advantages of the field over their heads:

- They have a too high BSA, which hosts microbes well for cycling and increases ration holding capacity.
- They can provide a piece, which is straightforward to select and move.
- They can be quite tough, easy to wash, and hard to compact.
- They can have a high void space, meaning good water movement.

➢ catches concrete without depositing them, meaning they will act in anaerobic areas. as a filter without generating.
➢ They can be natural or synthetic, made from recycled plastics, and reusable for many years.

CHAPTER 7: BIOLOGICAL FILTERS

Many aquaponics beginners are often confused with the need for filtration in their aquaponics system. Do I need a biofilter facility? This is one of the most asked questions in aquaponics. To answer the question, we wrote this text to debate biofilter, what it is, and your aquatic system needs to have one.

The idea behind aquaponics is that it is possible to mimic nature to create an ideal growing environment for fishes and plants to grow. Aquaponics can be a recycling method of farming that combines aquaculture and hydroponics, resulting in fish and plants grown together during symbiotic environments with beneficial bacteria. It converts the waste produced by the fish into nitrates, which become plant food and mutually filter the plant roots and clean the water for the fish. A biofilter helps ensure the process that nothing goes to waste.

What is a biofilter?

A biofilter can be the location of colonization of bacteria. It provides a large surface area, pH, dissolved oxygen level, and appropriate temperature.

Biofilters are simple to line up. They consist of a tank and some substrates connected to a vacuum pump to provide maximum volume in a large area for nitrifying bacteria to grow. The more room for bacterial growth, the higher because it means a more efficient nitrification process.

Biofiltration is the process of converting ammonia and nitrite into nitrate by beneficial bacteria. Ammonia and nitrite are toxic to aquatic organisms even at low concentrations. However, plants require nitrates to grow, so a biofilter must be installed to deal with most living bacteria. The motion of water within a biofilter will break down the excellent solids not captured, which prevents the useless formation of plant roots within the NXT aquaponics system. Good biofiltration is additionally necessary for the chemical stability of your bionomics system. Separate biofilters are unnecessary for media-based aquaponics systems because the growing beds themselves are the correct biofilters.

In Why Aquaponics Requires a Biofilter

If the area in your growth media is not sufficient to colonize bacteria, you want more area facilities. This is often why you want to be near a biofilter. The biofilter will form an essential part of your system to ensure that the plants have enough nutrients to stay healthy to measure water for fish.

Your entire aquaponics system can be a biofilter. However, if you are using the DWC, vertical, and NFT aquaponics systems to develop your plants, you will need a biofilter. In these aquaponics systems, you cannot trust the natural action of bacterial conversion due to a lack of sufficient area. A media-based or raft aquaponics system typically does not require a separate biofilter because the raft, growing media (expanded soil, gravel, or lava rock), tank walls, and other surface areas are sufficient to colonize bacteria. Provide area.

Benefits of using biofilter in aquaponics

1. It provides more area to measure beneficial bacteria and helps in converting ammonia and nitrite to nitrate.

2. Biofilter assists aeration and nitrification processes within NXT, DWC, and vertical aquaponics systems.

3. Help within the chemical stability of your aquaponics system.

4. Very inexpensive and straightforward to make.

5. Extremely easy to use and requires little or no maintenance.

Important Factors

Think About Before Using a Biofilter Before choosing to use a biofilter in your aquaponics system, you want to remember those ideas.

Remove first

Solids biofilter are not for giant solid fish waste. Solids should be investigated as this may block pipes. Once these solids accumulate in your biofilter, it can create an area referred to as an anaerobic zone that will attract bacteria and reduce your biofilter area. This may reduce your biofilters efficiency, which may end up in high ammonia levels, which are not suitable for fish and plants. Therefore, it is vital that you simply add a specific filter that will remove the solid.

Bacteria require air

In an aquaponics system, bacteria are exposed to air. Adding a biofilter to your aquaponics system will contain bacteria within the filter. Therefore, you must ensure that your filter has a sufficient air supply to ensure that bacteria are not out of the air.

Fish density

If you are running coffee fish density, you do not need a biofilter. There will not be sufficient production of small quantities of fish to justify the use of biofilter. The roots of the plant will provide enough area for the bacteria to convert ammonia into nitrate.

How does biofilter work in aquaponics?

The biofilter is an extension of the field of your aquaponics system. This is an essential part of your aquaponics system because it ensures that your plants can access the nitrates they have to grow while cleaning the fish's water. The bacteria will attach to the surface of your biofilter media. Once established, they are doing their job and help convert ammonia and nitrite to nitrate.

In aquaponics, biofiltration takes place in three main stages. This process is for commonly found aquaponics. The method or step may vary in count on your biofilter design.

1. The vacuum pump pumps water out of the aquarium and into the biofilter.

2. Inside the biofilter, water undergoes the nitrification process. Beneficial bacteria help convert ammonia and nitrite into nitrates.

3. Nutrient-filled water escapes from the biofilter into the plants, where the plant roots absorb nutrients when they clear the water before going back to the aquarium.

There are many different aquaponics biofilters biofilter that you can simply use in your aquaponics system;

These are:

Moving bed filter

This biofilter is employed during a floating raft system where there are not many areas for bacteria.

Static filters

These are tray-like filters slid into a separate container next to the aquarium before the plants. These provide an outdoor area for bacteria to collect. This filter must be positioned after the solid filter before reaching the plants, allowing the water to be filtered before reaching the plants.

Drip Filter

This filter allows water to drop from the highest. The water passes through the filter box, filled with gravel, oyster shells, or many other areas in a similar bio medium. This biofilter should also be placed where the water is filtered before reaching the plants. As the water moves through the filter, ammonia is converted into nitrates before being pumped back into the plants.

CHAPTER 8: FISH STOCKING

Closure of high-density stocks means high risk in aquaculture and aquaponics. Even commercial producers avoid high fish stocking densities, where the risk overtakes the return. Certainly, homemakers are best to avoid this at the least cost because it is simply not worthwhile.

Many refer to the high fish stocking density number of 1 fish in 10 liters of water. This number of fish is achievable in quarantine systems, with fingerings and tanks in place to eject them. However, you will not survive them at high density for a long time unless you have received severe filtration.

Newcomers to backyard aquaculture and aquaponics are being informed about what percentage of fish must be added and planted in their systems. To further complicate this, there is a clumsy explanation of why you would share the number of this fish. Throughout this article, I will be able to provide you with a less uncomfortable reason why you should not try these 100 fish in a 1000-liter reception.

So, what percentage of fish do you have?

How much fish you want to grow or what percentage of fish you want is the first thing on your plate. At home, this may depend on what percentage of fish you want from each hebdomadally and the way you are feeding. If you are trying for commercial growth, it can be ascertained what proportion of fish you will sell for a year and your production cost. For this example, we will use 50 fish.

The next thing to think about is how big you would like your fish to be. Suppose you want to eat 500 grams of fish each. A fish weighing 500 grams can be a typical market size for many species because they are considered "plate sizes." Some are small, some are big, but you compromise on it, so it is up to you. If you are growing to sell fish, then the dimensions are being given to customers to shop.

Then the tricky part is that you will weigh the amount of water per share of fish. This is often the stocking density factor expressed as kg / m3 or lbs. / ft3 depending on which side of the earth you are on. Converting backward and forward between these two is straightforward multiplication. Multiply lbs. / f3 = kg / m3 by 0.0624 and kg / m3 = lbs. / ft3 for solicitation by 16.02.

Avoid High Fish Stocking Density!

It is difficult to give comprehensive, general advice on density without knowing how your system is put together. The three primary criteria below will improve the number of fish you grow and feed well, and each of the three is associated with the oxygen supply to your fish tank:

Do you have a minimum aquarium of 1 to 1.5 timers per hour Water is exchanged?
Do you have enough aeration from air boulders or water return?
Do you remove fish solid waste and uncontrolled food using direct solids filtration?
If you have got the primary one, then fair water exchange 10kg / m3 or 0.63lbs / f3 will be ideal.

If you got aeration and water exchange, then 15kg / m3 or 0.94lbs / ft3 would work well.

If you have got all three, you will be ready to gain 25 kg / m3 or 1.56 lbs. / ft3.

"You will be surprised at what proportion your system will be more productive than solid filtration. Even basic. "

Achievable above 25 kg / m3, provided you tick all the boxes, and solid filtration improves. As a beginner, you want to move away from the upper density until you have grown some fish and understand your system and its limitations.

Now that you have understood your target density, how simple is the ratio of the aquarium you want. We will use 25kg / m3 or 1.56lbs / ft3 to continue our example.

How to make it all work

If you are performing from a known tank volume for 1000 liters. When working, it is crucial to assess the amount of water in the tank. Avoid the error of thinking a 1000-liter IBC can be a 1000-liter aquarium. If you reduce it, your IBC may have water below 100 mm high (freeboard), holding only 850 liters of water.

Working with the volume of the tank, the amount of the 1000 liters of water you are employing the volume of fish in this way: (1m3) Density factor (25 kg / m3) divided by the weight of the fish in multiplication (0.5 kg) (0.5 Kg) will present you. The number of fish to stock with. In this example = 50 fish.

Working with fish variety is the fish number (100) multiplied by the crop weight (0.5) of the fish divided by the density factor (25 kg / m3). You will need at least 2m3 or 2000 liters. Is the best.

There are various other environmental conditions, fish sizes, and conditions that indicate what percentage of fish you will give to your tank. Kind of like bio-filtration, but I think you have enough bed space or a purpose-built bio filter size.

Sticking to the fundamentals of 1 fish in 20 liters or less water, you will see many fish harvesting. Always add more tanks and keep your fish in the absolute best environment, and they will still produce a great product/food.

CHAPTER 9: FISHS

Aquaponics is a replacement term that many people hear nowadays; aquaponics can combine the two words aquaculture (raising aquatic animals) and hydroponics (plants growing in water). Aquaponics may thus be a method during which there are a depth and future biological relationship between marine animals and plants, where they both enjoy each other.

In aquaculture, fish waste accumulates in the water and increases the water's toxicity, causing damage to the fish. Hydroponics requires an endless supply of nutrients to plants that, in many cases, are not organic. So, to highlight this, aquaponics came into play, with aquaculture water fed into the hydroponic system. Here plants hunt fish waste as nutrients and thus purify the water and reduce toxicity. This toxin-free water is then pumped into aquaculture.

Fish play an essential role within the aquaponic system. The excreta of fish are employed as nutrients for plant growth. We want to think about some factors while selecting fish for the aquaponic system is not suitable for all fish to aquaponics. Most rules or elements need to be kept in mind:

Temperature - Firstly, when selecting a fish, and must be prepared to survive within your area's weather. Fishes are primarily cold-blooded animals, which means that they do not control the heat of their blood. Instead, they are dependent on the external environment they are in to manage their blood's heat. Therefore, the temperature of the climate is essential for the selection of fish.

Hot water fishes thrive in temperatures> 65oF a <85oF. Standard desirable water fishes are tilapia, catfish, bass, etc. If the temperature falls below 50oF, the tilapia will die. If your climate is on the cold side, these fish are not the right choice for aquaponics.

Coldwater fishes thrive in the temperature range of 50oF to 60oF. Coldwater fish are various trout species. The simplest rainbow trout to use in aquaponics is

Easy Availability - The next substantial interest when selecting fish is the limited availability of fish in your mind. For example, Barramundi is not readily available in the US, but it is readily available in Australia.

So, the simple acquisition of fingerplays also matters when selecting fish for aquaponics. Now tilapia are the most used fish for aquaponics as they are readily available in most parts of the planet. China is the largest producer of tilapia.

Which fish are legal in your area? This is often another essential factor to think about when starting aquaponics; it is not lawful for all fish to be bought and grown in some places. So, we must first check and confirm that the fish you will only use in aquaponics is legal in your business.

Even though tilapia is treated as fish common to aquatic organisms, they are considered pests in many countries due to the high prevalence rate. This overgrowth can lead to explanations for diseases that result in many of These species being banned in countries.

Tilapia

Temperature - Hot water fish, tolerant temperature 65oF to 85oF. Aquaponic systems are usually kept at 73 ° F to accommodate plants.

Availability - They are hardy fish; survival rates are high. They will withstand pH changes, ammonia level changes and eat the given feed. Indigo and Mozambique tilapia is the most preferred variety, as they have high growth rates and reproduction rates.

Legitimacy - Legal in most parts of the planet. They are considered an invasive species in the US, Australia, and South Africa. It is deemed illegal in some parts of the earth, so ask your state fisheries department before purchasing.

Trout

Temperature - These are cold-water fish; the ideal temperature required for them is 58oF - 68oF. They survive the season. The most desirable species of trout for aquaponics is rainbow trout. They are also popular aquaponic species grown in garages and cellars. Unlike trattoria, trout cannot handle dirty water.

Availability - Thanks to their cold-water habitat, they are not readily available in hot climatic zones. They are found within the natural habitats of North America, North Asia, and Europe.

Legitimacy - Even though they are not suitable for raising in many parts of the planet, trout farming is banned in many countries.] For example, trout farming has been banned in New Zealand because they fear it may be recreational trout fish May threaten adherence.

Perch

Temperature - The ideal temperature for perch is 70 to 82 degrees Fahrenheit. They thrive in hot water, but they will withstand water temperatures up to 50 degrees Fahrenheit.

Availability - They are edible, hardy, and adaptable aquaponic fishes. Popular types of perch are silver, yellow, and jade. They require a fair distribution throughout the planet. Jade perch is quickly available in Australia, but the most difficult to find outside in the US perc flavones are most used in aquaponics. They require only moderate temperatures and can withstand a wide pH range.

Legitimacy - Perch farming is legal in most parts of the planet, and perch fishing can be a recreational sport for many countries.

Catfish

Temperature - The ideal temperature for catfish is 78 to 86 degrees Fahrenheit. They thrive in hot water and are sensitive to sudden water temperature changes.

Availability - They feed aquaponic fish from below. They require pristine water, and pH should also be ideal. They live in water fishes and inland or coastal waters of all continents except Antarctica.

Legitimacy - Catfish farming is legal in most parts of the planet. In 2017 India banned African catfish as it posed a threat to native aquatic species.

Barramundi

Temperature - The ideal temperature is 78 to 83 degrees Fahrenheit. They thrive in hot water and overgrow.

Availability - They are edible aquaponic fish. Popular in Australia but raised in Singapore, Saudi Arabia, India, Indonesia, etc., they will be stored in freshwater and saltwater. Larger fishes will eat smaller fishes, so the breeding of fingerings is difficult. They have good quality water and very dissolved oxygen.

Legitimacy - Barramundi farming is legal in most parts of the planet. Their meat is exceptionally high priced and rich in omega-three carboxylic acids.

Bass

Temperature - The ideal temperature for bass is 75 to 85 degrees Fahrenheit. They thrive in warm water, but they are not hardy and friendly due to other species. They will tolerate low tide temperatures.

Availability - The top aquaponic bass varieties are Largemouth, Smallmouth, and Striped Bass. They are readily available as they are considered game fish in many places. Hybrid striped bass are favorable for aquaponics because they are flexible for temperature changes.

Legitimacy - They are legal in many parts of the planet but are considered invasive species in many places, such as Canada and North America.

Crustaceans

Temperatures - ideal temperatures for prawns are 82 to 88oF, lobster 71– 76oF, oyster 75 - 79oF. They will be grown alongside other fishers or separately. Red Claves can be a rapidly increasing crayfish for temperate climates, and nabob and marron are best suited for cooler temperatures.

Availability - Crustaceans are readily available in one part of the planet. They will be trouble-free as they are mostly feeders or filter feeders. They help keep the system clean

Aquatic - Crustacean farming is legal in most parts of the planet and fragile in many countries.

Any

Availability - They have gained popularity as ornamental fish in many parts of the planet. They are readily available but are a touch on the expensive side. They have high resilience to parasites and diseases.

Legalities - Some farming is legal in most parts of the planet, and they are mainly cultivated for ornamental purposes. They require a long lifetime of about 60 years.

Temperature - The ideal temperature for a Koi is 65 to 75 degrees Fahrenheit. These are the most popular ornamental fish.

Goldfish

temperature - The ideal temperature for goldfish is 68 to 75 degrees Fahrenheit. They are harsh and adapt to different water conditions. Rapid temperature changes are often fatal to them.

Validity - Goldfish farming is ultimately a part of the planet, and they are mainly cultivated for ornamental purposes. They require a long lifetime of about 15 years. They produce a lot of beneficial nutrients for the aquaponic system.

Availability - They need to fully gain popularity as ornamental fish that are a part of the planet. They are small and supply a lot of nutrients. Thanks to the small size, they are vulnerable to parasites.

Carp

Temperature - The ideal temperature for carp is 80 to 82 degrees Fahrenheit.
They thrive in hot water.
They are oily seafood.
They are popular in aquaculture.

Availability - They are mainly available in parts of the planet. However, in Western Europe, the increased cultivation of trout, salmon, etc. species has reduced their demand -

They are legitimate in many parts of the planet. They require good reproductive capabilities and can survive in most environments.

CHAPTER 10: BEST PLANTS

Tomatoes

The humble tomato performs exceptionally well during this water-based system. You will find it easier to control the temperature, and the amount of sun will also get to the plants.

However, it is worth noting that tomato plants are attracted to pests, which can be exceptionally difficult to avoid.

The leafy lettuce

Lettuce grown in aquaponics is one of the most leading producing leafy greens in the aquaponics system. Leafy lettuce will thrive in water, with temperatures between 70 and 74.

All you want to do is decide whether you are starting your seedbed or germinating seeds directly in the aquaponics system.

However, it will be beneficial to prevent seed loss in your growing media. Lettuce is suitable for growing in aquaponics if you are a beginner.

Watercress

This tough vegetation is one of the simplest plants for aquaponics because it overgrows. You will plant the same small plant, and it will grow amazingly.

However, you should consider whether it is often the simplest for you. There is only so much watercress you will eat. Its ability to multiply can offer you simultaneous issues with your growing bed, which can become clogged.

Pepper

Developing through a quality approach and quality gardening is exceedingly tricky. This is often because they are particularly aware of the water they consume and require a lot of sunlight.

It is sensible to develop them during a small aquaponics system. You will be ready to monitor your outdoor temperature and confirm the level of nutrients in your water. But more impressively is the ability to supply extremely hot chilies as you will correct the temperature dial for them.

It is worth noting that chili is not the best during a DWC aquaponic system. However, they are doing exceptionally well if you employ a flood and drain system.

It is worth noting that a flood and drain approach would require the use of a bell siphon.

Cucumbers

You already know what a cucumber is, but do you know that it is one of the simplest plants for aquaponics? An aquaponics system gives them everything they need to thrive, not just to survive.

Cucumbers possess extensive root systems; You must watch your pipes and siphons to ensure they do not attack and block them.

They are also good at accumulating nitrogen, possibly depriving other plants in your system. For this reason, it is a simple idea to offer an area between 30 and 60 cm between your plants and avoid overplanting. It is better to start with a couple of them and grow your system within the future.

Cauliflower

Cauliflower is another water-based plant that thrives in an aquaponics system.

These plants are very hardy and are wished for little or no maintenance. They are also generally resistant to insects and diseases. If you are a beginner, then it is one of the simplest plants in aquaponics.

Cauliflower should be able to be harvested in about 12 weeks. However, it does not like direct sunlight or frost. To avoid damage, it is best to hide at the top with your leaves; This can help make it even more significant.

Cabbage

Cabbage can be a staple food in many diets of the world. It is another right plant for aquaponics. You will need a pH range between 6.2 and 6.6 with temperatures between 60 and 70 ° F.

In general, this plant requires little or no maintenance. The most critical issue is when the apex is divided; You must keep an eye to ensure that dirt and disease do not enter the cabbage through these splashes.

Also, you must focus on common pests, Aphids, fungal disease, and plant disease.

Ideally, your seedlings should be kept a touch warmer than your mature crop; This can encourage them to grow. Cabbage is often able to harvest in nine weeks.

Strawberries

These little red fruits are great for eating all year round. (Technically, a strawberry is not a fruit, vegetable, or berry but is a remarkable story). It is often an excellent aquaponics plant to grow in your system. Due to the continuous supply of nutrient-rich water and their ability to regulate the environment, plants do not realize that it is winter, meaning that you will harvest all year round.

To grow strawberries in the aquaponics system, you must plant more and more plants. This is often because most plants will only produce a pair of strawberries; If you want to enjoy eating them or perhaps sell them; Then you will want to keep many plants to grow.

The good news is that every plant needs little or no space, and you will use floating fleet systems, tubes, or perhaps baskets. Strawberries require little or no care to flourish and are an excellent plant for the first-time cultivator.

Other Aquaponics Vegetables and Fruits:

If you are feeling adventurous about aquaponics, the latter are also excellent plants; You've got to monitor your environment carefully:

- Sweet Corn
- Beet
- Dwarf Sour
- Onion
- Radish
- Orchids
- Violas
- Microgreens
- Asparagus
- Wheatgrass
- Baking Choi
- Swiss Chard
- Arugula
- Chives
- Carrot
- Onion

CHAPTER 11: PEST

Natural Pest Control is an important consideration when setting it up Incorporated for and maintaining an aquaponics system. Keeping your aquaponic system organic is one way to ensure that the plants, fish, and food you cut are safe and edible. A lot of chemicals are often dangerous for fish and the people who work with them. Studies have shown a strong correlation between chemicals within the food system and many diseases and illnesses. You want to look for safe but effective types of natural pest control. To try to do this, you will want to understand your enemy pests, understand standard biological techniques to remove or destroy pests, and the way beneficial insects can work wonders in your aquaponic garden.

Aquaponic pests in the aquaponic monsoon the system, problems are often as large as a drag for other gardening or farming methods. Often "> This is often true of outdoor or backyard setups, although it can be a problem indoors as well. Aquaponic pests are indistinguishable from your typical garden pests, and that they can cause some severe damage to your plants. harm can come and so flower., fruit, or vegetables they produce several the worst pests' criminals:

APHIDS

CATERPILLARS

TOMATO HORNWORMS

COLORADO POTATO BEETLES

MEALYBUGS

CUTWORMS

SQUASH VINE BORERS

SQUASH BUG

VARIOUS PLANT-EATING BEETLES

Theatre insects and their entire crop Can be eliminated if not handled properly, but using pesticides is often an actual problem in an aquaponic system. However, organic gardening does not focus your attention. The harsh chemicals and poisons found in most pesticides are often associated with your fish. Are extremely dangerous.

So how are insects prevented from destroying their plants while keeping them? Is your fish safe? You are doing this with proven organic gardening methods. Safely eliminating the number of pests or There are many well-documented reasons for reducing Reek. Who are attacking your plants? Start by checking the plants regularly for pests. Hand removal will work wonders for problems that appear on your plants. Just pick up any insects you see and destroy them. This is often quite labor-intensive, so using hand removal combined with other methods is a simple idea. One popular way that is used in both aquaponics and traditional methods is the use of insect-repellent plants. Some plants drive the insects away, and you will plant them with the plant you want to grow. You will plant artemisias, nasturtiums, catnip, dill, chrysanthemum, chives, petunias, peppermint, and as a kind of natural pest control.

Another simple organic gardening method you will use in your aquaponic system is bug netting. This creates a physical barrier between the plants and can prevent many pests from entering. This method works indoors and outdoors, but regular inspection of plants is strongly recommended. You will also investigate non-pesticide ways of destroying insect populations. Glue traps are available and can be used during your aquaponic system's growing beds to catch insects. The only drawback is that these traps will catch pests that you only want to keep near pollinators and other beneficial bugs. This brings us to a different common technique to eliminate problems that you can use helpful insects.

Beneficial pests

Bringing some pests that get plant-damaging species into your aquaponic system is an excellent way of biological pest control. Many insect varieties are happy enough to make food from problems that are munching on your plants. You will attract these profitable varieties by creating a pleasant habitat for them. Most species that eat garden pests are easily attracted to flowers. In some cases, especially with indoor systems, you must give nature a hand by adding the supporting insect species yourself.

You will buy insect-munching insects or find them outside yourself and deliver them to your system. Some beneficial insects that are a great type of natural pest control for your aquaponic system:

Ladybugs / Lady Beetles - Both adult and larval types of these little ones can work wonders when destroying garden pests. They eat aphids, small beetles and caterpillars, and most insect eggs. Some species also eat mealybugs, mites, and other soft-bodied insects. They will again eat mildew, which is another common problem in aquaponic systems.

Lacewing - The larvae of lacewing eat almost everything from aphids to caterpillars to mile bugs. They are also quite keen on insect eggs and other larvae. Adults of the species are also known to eat other insects, although their favorite food is nectar.

Spiders - Although not technically an insect, these creatures are great at keeping insect populations. Even young or small spiders can do an excellent job of eating insects that destroy your plants. Anything that finds its way into its web, including caterpillars, aphids, moths, cutworms, squash bugs, and budworms.

Tachinid flies - their larvae can eat caterpillars, cat worms, squash bugs, beetles, ear wives, and even grasshoppers. Adults are also known to eat other insects but generally prefer nectar and pollen, making them excellent pollinators.

Ground beetle - Adults of this species are quite large, and the only one can eat quite a few garden pests. They will help keep slugs and snails, cutworms, caterpillars, potato beetles, squash borers, root maggots, and budworms in check. Soldier beetle is another similar species that provides a similar advantage.

With a tactile effort, it is entirely possible to keep insects from destroying your aquatic plants without doing any harm to your fish or yourself within the process. Avoiding pesticides and those who specialize in natural pest control methods will help ensure your aquaponic system's success. You will continue to damage pests outside your garden with preventive procedures such as planting insect-resistant plants or using nets or nets. You will also use some beneficial bugs that will help prevent harmful insects from eating them. By employing a combination of those methods, you will be ready to run your system smoothly and achieve a healthy harvest.

CHAPTER 12: SYSTEM DESIGN

Mainly, three different types of aquaponics system design: Nutrient Film Technique (NXT), Media Bed, and Trouble Culture (DWC). Although these are not the only three designs, they are still the most common, and here is what we use in ECOLIFE. When deciding what type of system to build, it is crucial to weigh every design's pros and cons to fit your needs and capability best.

It is essential to trust the intended use of the system. Whether it is for personal, educational, or commercial use, your intentions will ultimately determine what the need for a calm system is.

What is the ratio of space/scale: space? Does anyone get to maximize this? In what proportion, for whom, and for what purpose will the production take place?

Crop Type: You must match the system to the crops. Temperature range, nutrient demand, growth rate, weight, and root zone are essential design selection factors.

Environment: Annual, seasonal, and daily temperature fluctuations will directly affect the productivity of various life forms and, ultimately, the planning of your system. Would you like to soak or exchange heat? Is it in or out?

Technical capabilities: Each design has characteristics that lend themselves to different levels of experience. Who will use and manage it, and how food production and aquaculture techniques are realized?

NUTRIENT film technology

Best use:

NFT systems are popular within the commercial industry due to their space efficiency and low labor costs. Because crops can also be grown on a vertical plane (or shelf), they are easily accessible and crop able. Warm with hydroponic production, this method is best applied to leafy greens. This design has not been applied to large fruitful plants because their core mass may block the channel, and their weight cannot be supported. Plant roots are exposed to more air and less water in the NXT system, making plants susceptible to extreme heat or cold fluctuations.

Media bed

like containers uses a media aquaponics bed Like gravel or expanded soil (hydro ton) to support plants' roots crammed with rock media. The bed is replenished to provide nutrients and oxygen to the plants and drainage of nutrient-rich water. The media wants to support plants as both a mechanical and biofertilizer to capture and break up waste.

BEST USE

This technique is best used for backyard gardeners and beginners as it does not require engineering, aquaponics, or plant science background to function well. It is inexpensive, simple to place together, and is small-scale productive. Because the media supports plants such as soil, you are ready to produce large, rooted plants such as fruits, flowering plants, vegetables, and conventional vegetables. Because media is not space-efficient and requires exceptionally high labor inputs, media bed designs are widespread in commercial use.

Professionals in larger crops wells baht biofiltration cheap applying for simple WRKO work right small-scale Pinelike Lehman

CONS
- difficult the scale of mass production
- require than cleaning
- higher maintenance and labor

Deep water culture (DWC)

Also referred to as a raft or boat system, this method uses floating rafts to suspend plant roots in nutrient-rich and aerated waters. The origins of the plant float directly in a pool of water up to about 1 foot. Since there are no media to capture and process solid waste, filtration techniques must be built into the plan. This necessitates more advanced aquaculture techniques and system requirements, resulting in higher upfront costs.

BEST USE

This design is standard with commercial production because it is the most stable of the three system types. Because there is far more water within the system, harsh nutrients and temperature fluctuations are much less likely. It is best for warm climates because it can resist daily temperature swings, but it is expensive to heat water in cold climates. Additionally, large root zone plants are often used, and plants' removal is much easier than in media beds.

ECOLIFE aquaponics program uses ECOLIFE aquaponics demand, a type of sustainable agriculture that uses Does 90% less water, a space fraction, and does not require traditional agriculture's chemical and energy inputs. Aquaponics allows us to grow anywhere, including urban food deserts, classrooms, and community meeting centers. We are helping to end food insecurity in San Diego so that year-on-year access to healthy produce is available to those who need it most. In and out of the classroom, ECOLIFE's educational programming trains young students to train professionals and teach the community about aquaponics' social and environmental benefits.

Our ECO-Cycle Aquaponics Kit engages students in food system innovation and science at an early age. Our community garden aquaponics system provides agricultural workforce development while supplying healthy, sustainable production. Finally, our Aquaponics Innovation Center is a signaling and research center to advance and spread Aquaponics best practices.

Where We Work

Classroom: ECOLIFE has donated 658 aquaponics kits to classrooms across the state, educating more than 120,000 students. The K-12 NGSS curriculum engages students with their food systems, highlighting the challenges of industrial food systems that build tutorial infrastructure for a sustainable future.

Communities: We have built ten community garden systems in schools and community centers in San Diego, spreading knowledge about sustainable agriculture and building supplies.

The Farm: Aquaponics Innovation Center is ECOLIFE's 3,000-gallon small-scale commercial demonstration and research system. In 8 months, we have produced 1,138 pounds and hosted a 1910-hour job.

CHAPTER 13: SUMMING UP AQUAPONICS

One of the most important ways of growing food is aquaponics. It consists of a mixture of aquaculture and hydroponics in an integrated system. Once you find out, little or no maintenance or effort is required.

The basic premise of aquaponics is that the waste produced by your fish feeds the plants, and therefore the plants clean the water for the fish, creating a continuous cycle.

This system is wholly dedicated to biological processes. When fish produce waste (ammonia), bacteria break it down into nitrates. A pump then carries this water, high in nitrates, to the growing bed where the plants are growing. Plants draw nitrogen from the water, which feeds the plants and cleans the water, making it safe to return to the aquarium.

This cycle repeatedly repeats, with the fish providing nutrition for the bacteria, the bacteria break down the fish waste and feed the plants, so the plants clean the water to return the fish. Easy!

Why does food grow like this?

Aquaponics uses less water than other horticulture by at least one-tenth of the amount used in traditional soil-based gardening.

Aquaponics requires less time than regular fishing, as the plants do many cleaning tasks for you.

Growing up with aquaponics is entirely biological. You cannot just use any harsh chemicals, as they are going to be fatal to fish.

Aquaponics growing beds are usually waist high; as you move towards your plants, the stress on your back decreases.

As with other types of food gardening, the amount of time you must grow with aquaponics is meager.

Food is often grown anywhere: indoors, in a greenhouse, even in your bedroom!

The system is often adapted to your needs - small enough to feed something or large to provide a community.

Aquaponics Design: Which System Is Best?

There are alternative methods to line the aquaponics system. The three most common are:

Deep Water Culture Detected

Trouble Culture System, additionally referred to as fleet-based mounting, uses a floating fuel raft commonly used in large commercial setups. This allows the plant roots to fall into the water and pull nutrients directly from the channel that is running through the water. The water will be drained from the tank where the fish lives and has been filtered to eliminate any solid waste.

This method involves drawing water from the aquarium through a narrow, cylindrical tube such as PVC, with holes drilled most. Roots are endangered through pores, where they draw nutrients from the water. This works for too high ground areas, as they often meet walls or hang from the ceiling. It is usually found horizontally or vertically and is excellent for plants that do not require any support to grow, like leafy greens.

Media beds detected

In this system, plants are grown during a specific type of media such as soil pebbles, and therefore the media bed usually sits above or next to the aquarium. A pump draws water from the tank, and then it passes through the media bed, allowing the plants to pull nutrients from the water before it returns to the fully filtered fish.

DIY Aquaponics in Five Easy Steps

Here is how to explore an aquaponics system that will allow you to develop your food reception using a media bed system.

Step one: Keep your aquarium together

Like fish, you must consider all the safe practices of fishing. Your fish will need to count a particular amount of space on the species you choose, which can determine your tank's dimensions.

Depending on the dimensions of the tank you choose, you will likely be ready to run away with using or reusing a specific acrylic aquarium. However, most people prefer to use large barrels or food-grade containers with opaque sides.

You will need to install the tank as soon as you take a traditional fish tank out of the water and allow you to cycle between 4-6 weeks before adding any fish. This provides time for bacteria to grow, ensuring that the nitrates needed to feed your plants have enough present to inhibit ammonia and nitrite.

Be sure to include a pump, which allows water to drain from the tank, rise on the bed and return.

Step Two: Build Your Media Bed
Media beds can be built either above the aquarium or on the side of the tank.

Your media bed is going to be the container during which the plants grow. It is also often referred to as a flood table. You will use a heavy-duty plastic tray or wooden pallet crate. It can be built above a stand that is ready to withstand its weight.

Once you have a media bed, you need to fill it with your chosen media. Soil pebbles are pH neutral and will not affect your water. They also hold moisture well. For these reasons, they are one of the most popular types of media to use in-home aquaponics.

When you first start, stick to a ratio of 1: 1 between the aquarium's dimensions and, therefore, the size of the bed that grows so that the volumes are equivalent.

Step Three: Add Fish

Once your tank is appropriately cyclic, you will add fish.

There are a variety of different fishes that work well in aquaponics found outside. The general like:

TILAPIA - THE SIMPLE FISH-GROWING, EASY TO WORRY, AND TO
CREATE TONS OF HARDIE - WASTE ILLNESS, SO ARSHIA THIS
KOI- THEY GROW UP AND HIGH RESALE VALUE
PAK - THOSE TRYING TO FIND A

FISH FANATIC. ANY ORNAMENTAL FISH (GUPPIES, TETRAS, MOLLIES, ETC.)

Fewer standard options include:

CARP - REPRODUCE WELL AND ARE EASY TO GROW
SILVER PERCH - A FAST-GROWING SCHOOL FISH THAT PREFER HIGH DENSITY
CATFISH - DO NOT HANDLE THE SCALES. A MINIMUM MUST BE KEPT AT THE
BARRAMUNDI'S - PRINCE OF FISH IN THE WORLD OF AQUAPONICS.

Step four: Add plants.

Leafy plants grow best in aquaponics setup. However, if you have enough fish, you will probably also be ready to grow fruiting plants such as peppers and tomatoes.

Here is a list of some easy-to-grow plants for your system:

- Basil
- Banana
- Lettuce

- Mint
- Watercress

You can also get these plants ready to grow if you are heavily stocked and well established:

- Beans
- Cabbage
- Cauliflower
- Cucumbers
- Squash
- Tomatoes
- Peas
- Peppers
- Strawberries

It is best to transplant your plants for a start. Place your roots gently into the pebble, ensuring that they reach far enough down to pull nutrients from the water that will pass through.

Step Five: Your system is Finding Straightforward!

It would be best if you fed your fish a high-quality diet. You will use an easy crust food and provide them with topical treatment. Just take care that you do not introduce any disease in the tank. For this reason, we advise against adding any live food to the fish.

Only feed your fish in maximum quantities as they will provide for about five minutes, two to 3 times per day.
You must test the tank's water two or more times to see the pH, ammonia, nitrite, and nitrate levels. Ammonia and nitrite levels must be non-detectable, nitrite must be reduced when plants do their job correctly!

Between 6.8 - 7.0, the pH should be neutral, accurate for fish, plants, and therefore bacteria.

Aquaponics systems usually must be buffered because they will fall below 7.0 after the initial cycle ends. To boost the pH, you will alternate between lime and carbonate to be added to the powder form tank.

Combine the plants with your standard gardening techniques, but you should find that weeds do not grow that much.

CHAPTER 14: TIPS AND TRICKS

From a media bed unit start-up in Bangkok to a fully-fledged 120 home trouble culture (DWC) unit in Ethiopia, Aquaponics delivers its actual ability to supply sustainable food anytime, anywhere Is demonstrating A marriage between aquaculture (raising aquatic animals such as fish, snails, or prawns in water) and hydroponics (cultivating plants in water) can be a 'clean and green' way to nurture plants in aquaponics recycling systems efficiently is.

To date, 150 different vegetables, herbs, flowers, and small trees have been successfully grown in aquaponic systems, including domestic and commercial units.

Whether you are starting your aquaponics unit reception, developing a large-scale aquaponics project, or championing small-scale aquaponic units within the classroom, here are seven rules to follow: choose the

Tank carefully. Fish tanks are an essential component in every aquaponic unit. Any aquarium will work, but round tanks with flat or conical bottles are recommended because they are easy to clean. Remember: Due to their durability and long lifetime, try to use strong passive plastic or fiberglass tanks.

Ensure adequate aeration and water circulation. This shows you that you should use water and air pumps to ensure a fair amount of dissolved oxygen and water in the water so that your animals, bacteria, and plants are healthy. Remember: The cost of electricity is a big part of the system budget, so choose the pumps and the power source wisely and consider photovoltaic power if possible.

Maintain good water quality. Water is the lifeblood of an aquaponic system. It is the medium through which all essential nutrients are transported to the plants, which is where the fish live. It is crucial to observe and control five major water quality standards: dissolved oxygen (5 mg/liter), pH (6–7), temperature (18–30 °C), total nitrogen, and water alkalinity. Remember: Water chemistry may seem complicated, but specialized management is comparatively simple with available test kits.

Do not overthrow the tanks. If stocking density is kept low, your aquaponic system can easily manage and remain untouched against shocks and collapse. The recommended stocking density is 20 kg / 1 000 liters, leaving the plant growing area. Remember: Higher stocking densities can produce more food in one place but require far more active management. Avoid over-breastfeeding and remove any unused food. Waste and raw food are very harmful to aquatic animals because they will rot inside the system. Rotting food can cause illness, and all dissolved oxygen can be spent. Remember: feed the animals one day, but do not remove any food after half an hour and then adjust the portion of the day after.

Choose and keep plants wisely. Plant vegetables with low growing duration (salad greens) between plants with long duration crops (brinjals). Continuous replication of tender vegetables such as lettuce among large fruitful plants provides a naturally shaded condition. Remember: Generally, leafy green plants do very well in aquaponics, along with several of the most popular productive vegetables, including tomatoes, cucumbers, and peppers.

Maintain a balance between plants and animals. Employing a batch cropping system can help keep a uniform crop of both aquatic animals and vegetables to maintain a consistent production level and a constant balance between fish and plants. Remember: Safe source of young plants and young is essential, so confirm that availability is considered during the design phase.

CONCLUSION

As a result of our collected data, we had to contend with our data's two different conclusions. We observed that the aquaponic system considered tomato plants better than normal garden plants during the expansion and progress of tomato plants. Because of our choices and actions, our experiment resulted in this way, everyone's project will have a particular result or will be different from each other. We believe that tomato plants within the aquaponic system are healthier and more robust than conventionally planted tomatoes due to natural nutrients. We all know that the aquaponic system has many benefits that will improve plants. There are many advantages; Nitrite is changing to nitrate, ammonia, and therefore pH, which is being transferred from the aquarium to the plant box. We believe tomato plants are well dressed and healthy due to those nutrients.

www.ingramcontent.com/pod-product-compliance
Lightning Source LLC
Chambersburg PA
CBHW070904080526
44589CB00013B/1175